SPEECH

OF

HON. HENRY M. FULLER,

UPON

THE CONTESTED ELECTION

FROM THE

ELEVENTH CONGRESSIONAL DISTRICT OF PENNSYLVANIA,

HENDRICK B. WRIGHT *vs.* HENRY M. FULLER.

DELIVERED IN THE HOUSE OF REPRESENTATIVES, JUNE 25, 1852.

WASHINGTON:
PRINTED BY JNO. T. TOWERS.
1852.

SPEECH

OF

HON. HENRY M. FULLER,

UPON THE

CONTESTED ELECTION FROM THE ELEVENTH CONGRESSIONAL DISTRICT OF PENNSYLVANIA.

DELIVERED IN THE HOUSE OF REPRESENTATIVES, JUNE 25, 1852.

Mr. FULLER addressed the House as follows:

Mr. SPEAKER: Before I proceed with my argument, I wish to inquire of the Chair what is the usual course pursued in proceedings of this character? I know the contestant is present, and I understand he desires to be heard by the House in his own behalf. If that be the case, I wish to move that he be furnished with a seat upon the floor for that purpose.

The SPEAKER. The Chair decides that in very many cases contestants have been admitted to seats upon the floor, and been allowed to be heard in their own cases.

Mr. FULLER. I move, if the gentleman desires it, that he be permitted to do so in this case.

[Cries of "Agreed!" "Agreed!"]

The question was then taken upon Mr. FULLER's motion, and it was agreed to.

Mr. WRIGHT then took a seat within the bar.

Mr. FULLER. I have nothing to say for myself. I speak to-day in behalf of a majority of the people of the Eleventh Congressional District of Pennsylvania. Were I alone concerned this case would be submitted to your decision, without any remarks of mine. But, when the people of my district are unjustly accused, when they are arraigned and put upon their trial, it is not permitted that I, their elected Representative, should remain silent. This action makes it my duty to defend their reputation thus assailed, to vindicate the purity of their motives, and the fairness of their election; to repel all unworthy imputations, to wipe out all false aspersions upon their character and good name. In discharge of that duty, it will be my object fully and frankly to relate the history of this contest, and to state all the facts which have brought it before the House and before the country. The character of the case will require me to become somewhat personal, without intentional offense, however, and, of course, within the rules of parliamentary order; so far as there may be occasion to speak of myself, it will be done, I trust, with becoming modesty; and so far as there may be necessity to speak of others, it shall be done moderately, temperately, and with all possible charity.

Sir, four weeks previous to the election here in controversy, little dreamed I of becoming a candidate, much less of being elected to the present Congress; but it so happened, in the political history of the district, that the nomination of the honorable contestant was not altogether so satisfactory as it should have been. This, surely, was no fault of mine. It may not have been any fault of his, though I submit that such a state of feeling as existed there rarely arises without some real or supposed good and sufficient cause. What the reasons were that influenced the people on that occasion would not be the subject of legitimate inquiry here. The effects of the disease, however, will I think be sufficiently exposed without tracing the cause. Be that as it may, at the solicitation of many worthy and highly honorable men of both political parties, both Whigs and Democrats, I was induced to enter the canvass, and most unexpectedly, and I am frank to admit, quite as undeservedly, I was elected. I do not claim the election as the result of any merit or public service of mine. It would not become me to say that it was owing to any demerit on the part of my honorable opponent, but the fact is undoubtedly true that the people, in the exercise of their constutional right, chose to withdraw their confidence from him, and cast it, undeserved, upon me. Now, that he was greatly mistaken, that he was greatly disappointed, I have every reason to believe; for, only a few days before the election, he expressed his regret, in most decided terms, that he would be compelled to defeat me, his neighbor, so badly. This was very kind, most amiable, and most neighborly on his part. I remember to have rejoined in the same spirit, expressing my entire satisfaction with any result; but, at the same time, commending him to a prudent husbandry of all his resources. Now, that he was disappointed, I have still stronger reason to believe, for, on the very day of the election, up to the hour of the closing of the polls, he boasted very loudly, and most publicly, (as his habit is,) that his majority would be 2,999, with something to spare.

Had it been so, Mr. Speaker—had his expectations been realized, no man could have yielded more cheerfully than I would. Instead of being soured and disappointed, it would have rather rejoiced me that the people of the district had elected a man so much abler—certainly so much more *anxious*—to represent them than I. But had he been elected by one majority, I trust no man, neither he, nor any of his friends, will ever do me the injustice to suppose that I could have contested it. No, sir, I was prepared *then*, as I trust I am prepared now, to fall at least with decency. No, sir; my principles, such as they are, and my sense of duty, such as it is, have ever taught me to bow with respectful submission to the expressed will of the people; and desperate, indeed, in my humble judgment, must that man's political fortunes have become—reckless, indeed, of human evil and human peril must that man have become, who wantonly attempts to thwart the wishes, to palsy the will, or to set aside the verdict of the people; for rest assured, that "whom they will they will set up, and whom they will they will set down." Mr. Speaker, our experience in life proves the fact, that the philosophy of some men is unequal to discomforture. The public appreciation of men does not always quite come up to their own appreciation of themselves. It often happens with defeated candidates, whose aspirations for political preference have in some manner been signally disappointed, that they imagine themselves to have been greatly wronged, grossly cheated, infamously defrauded. Perhaps there is no man who shows this infirmity more largely than the honorable contestant himself. Now, in order to show you with what facility some men will deceive themselves in this particular, and in order to illustrate more fully this part of my argument, I propose to give you an example exactly in point, and I am induced to do so for the reason that the gentleman himself, in his opening speech before the committee, as they will remember, declared that this was the second time that he had been cheated out of a seat in this House.

In 1848 the gentleman was a candidate for Congress, and at that time ran in opposition to the late lamented Mr. Butler, a pure and upright man, as many of you know, and also against a Mr. Collings, as able and as unflinching a Democrat as is to be found in the State of Pennsylvania. On that occasion he was defeated, and immediately thereafter appeared in a newspaper, in which I believe he is largely interested, an article, which was said to have been written by himself. He will have an opportunity of denying it, if I misstate the matter; but taking it, as I do, to be his own production, and regarding it, therefore, as the highest authority, I read it for the information of the House. It is to this effect:

"SHAMEFUL FRAUD.—A most disgusting fraud occurred on the day of election in the Carbondale district. The Democratic tickets were folded up in bunches, and put in the hands of Mr. Thomas Boland for distribution at the polls. These tickets he carried in his coat pockets. The Federalists procured tickets in the same type, and tied them up in exact imitation of the Democratic bunches—and watching Mr. Boland in the crowd, took the tickets with Colonel Wright's name, out of his pockets, and placed the Whig ones in the place of them. Mr. Boland not discovering the error, handed out the bunches to the voters, who put them in the polls, supposing them to be the Democratic ticket, with Colonel Wright's name among them. In this way our Democratic candidate for Congress was defeated. Shame *where* is thy blush? When fraud of this kind is resorted to, can a cause prosper? We were well aware that Colonel Wright would get from one hundred and fifty to two hundred majority in the Carbondale district, and had he not been CHEATED in this way, would have been triumphantly elected over a stronger combination of men and money than was ever brought to bear against a single man before. But though defeated, he is at this moment stronger in the affections of the people of this district, than though he had been successful."

"THE FRAUD.—We cannot help again reverting to the revolting and wicked fraud in the Carbondale district. Our information is, that at least one hundred men went to the polls with, as they supposed, Colonel Wright's ticket in their hand, but were deceived and cheated out of their choice. What must an HONORABLE man *think*, who holds a place obtained in this way? Does he repose easy on his pillow, when the station he is elevated to is the result of so base a deception?

"We know it is no apology for a voter not to examine his tickets; but how many hundreds are there who take the tied up bunch from the hand of a friend? So it was done at Carbondale, and Mr. Boland all the time supposing he was handing out Colonel Wright's tickets—while craven villains were picking his pockets, and supplying them with other tickets. Are such frauds to prosper?"

Mr. STUART. I rise to a question of order. I understand the gentleman to be discussing circumstances attending an election two years prior to the one now in dispute.

Mr. FULLER. This is a mere illustration of my argument to show how men will be deceived in this respect.

The SPEAKER. Does the gentleman insist upon his point of order.

Mr. STUART. I do, sir.

The SPEAKER. The Chair does not know precisely the application of the paper which the gentleman is reading, which he adopts as part of his speech, and is disinclined to rule him out of order.

Mr. FULLER. I have read as much as I *desire*, and, although sustained by the *Speaker*, I will desist. The first scene in this drama of contested election opened just seven days after the canvass had closed, and came very near being a tragedy in the first act. Under the election laws of Pennsylvania the return judges, or canvassers of the several counties, are required to meet at a place designated by law for the purpose of footing up the returns, ascertaining the result, and giving to the individual chosen a certificate of his election. The judges met in pursuance of this law, on the seventh day after the election at the borough of Wilkesbarrre, where the honorable gentleman and myself both reside. Meanwhile, the lightning and the press had announced the result of the Pennsylvanian election all over the country, and I had the pleasure, if pleasure it could be, of seeing myself in print as the member elect from the eleventh Congressional district; and while in the very act of receiving the congratulations of my Whig and Democratic friends, who had elected me, while we were in the act of making ourselves merry in the manner and after the fashion of the times, what sort of an announcement do you think I received? Why, sir, I was told that the judges were in convention, and that the honorable contestant had presented himself before them, and was demanding, ay, begging, and that, too, tearfully, a certificate of his election. *Ex gratia modestiæ!* Before the election, claiming three thousand majority, and after the election, attempting to get a certificate by disfranchising just about the same number! Will he deny that? What was his argument? It was that Montour county, a new county, which had been erected out of a part of Columbia, then and now a part of the district, had not then held her courts, and that she was not entitled, therefore, to a separate representative in the board of returning officers. It was not contended, sir, that they had not the right to vote, nor was it contended that their vote was not correctly numerically returned, but upon this shallow pretence, this bald invention, this miserable quibble, did the gentleman attempt to disfranchise over two thousand voters.

On that occasion I remember to have heard one of the most remarkable speeches to which I ever listened in my life. One of the most remarkable, perhaps, in the history of human eloquence—for *pathos* and deep feeling, that of Mark Anthony, over the dead body of Cæsar, would bear no sort of comparison. Not content with pressing the legal argument, which he did with great force—he urged other considerations upon the attention of the judges. What these considerations were, I do not propose now to relate. They were innocent, however, and perhaps, to avoid all improper inferences, I may as well state, that he pressed upon them his age, that he was a native of the county, that his voice had been heard for twenty years in that court-house, that he had rendered many most important, but long, unrequited public services, and therefore, that he should have a certificate of election. But, sir, the judges, all of them Democrats, because every county in the District is strongly Democratic, would not, of course, yield to this extraordinary demand. They were men of firmness and integrity—they were men who felt that their oaths and their honor were of higher obligation than their duties as partisans, and as honest men, they of course refused; in this respect permit me to say, they have set a high and *worthy example.* Had it been otherwise, the honorable contestant might have taken a certificate, but it would have been against law—against the popular will, and in defiance of public shame. Had he received it he could not have retained it a single hour, for such would have been the excitement of a people, whose sentiments of common law, common honesty, and common justice, would have been outraged, that no earthly power could have prevented their doing themselves justice, even at the personal sacrifice of the contestant and the judges. Then there would have been a tragedy in the first act, and the harmony of this interesting drama very much disturbed. Fortunately the integrity of the judges averted any such result.

Now, sir, in order to show in what light this proceeding is regarded by the tried and true Democracy of the district, I propose to read from the leading Democratic journal, published in the very town where the contestant resides. That will be in order, I am sure. It is the Wilkesbarre Farmer and Journal:

"ELEVENTH CONGRESSIONAL DISTRICT.—The following is the official vote in this district:

	Wright.	*Fuller.*
Montour	473	1,717
Columbia	1,589	932
Luzerne	3,247	2,948
Wyoming	848	619
	6,157	6,216
		6,157
Fuller's majority		59

"The return judges of the district are now in session at the court-house in this borough. Strenuous opposition has been raised by the defeated candidate and his friends to the reception of the votes from Montour county, on the ground of alleged informality in the proceedings of the board of return judges of that county. The vote of Montour county is sought to be thrown out, and a constituency numbering between two and three thousand thus disfranchised. In such a proceeding as this, the true and faithful Democracy of this county have, and will have, no lot or part. They believe religiously in the sacred character of the right of franchise, and regard with abhorrence every effort of unscrupulous men, under the stimulus of bad passion and greedy ambition, to violate that right. They denounced the infamous frauds of the memorable era known as the 'buck shot war,' and they will not wheel about and be guilty of the same atrocities themselves. They know that the inviolability of this right rests at the very basis of all their civil and religious liberty; that upon it and an honest abidance by its decisions depends the security and the safety of their lives and property, and by no act of theirs will this sacred safeguard be broken down.

"The majority in the above case is clearly ascertained and expressed. The will of the people is made manifest in unmistakable unmbers, and no earthly tribunal has the right to set that will aside."

That, sir, is good Democratic doctrine in my district.

Having thus disposed of the early history of the case, we will proceed to reply to the argument of the honorable chairman of the Committee on Elections. Before proceeding further, however, I will state in this connexion, that the specifications of the contestant, some twelve in number, and very wide in their latitude, were narrowed down to the single poll of the borough of Danville. Now, sir, how did the gentleman and myself stand related to this poll? I live, and he lives, fifty miles distant, and so brief was the period between my nomination and the election that I had no opportunity of visiting it all. In this respect the honorable contestant had very greatly the advantage; for it is in evidence, as the committee will remember, that he visited the borough of Danville under the happiest possible auspices, at the invitation of Captain Thomas Brandon, who appears, from this evidence, to have been his particular friend, adviser, and correspondent. It was at his written request that the contestant visited the borough of Danville, and while there, he was engaged in rallying his friends, in giving all the required pledges upon their local questions, and in making such distribution of the "material aid" as is usual, and which he regards as exceedingly potent in campaigns of this character. [Laughter.] But such was the effect (I will not, however, charge the gentlemen with producing it) upon Captain Thomas Brandon, that it is in evidence here that he became, on the day of the election, most strangely unmindful of his duty as a good citizen. It is in evidence here that Captain Thomas Brandon voted number ten in the morning, and becoming oblivious to that fact, attempted to vote number four hundred and forty-eight in the afternoon. [Laughter.] Such is the fact, sir. It will not be denied. And I allege that this is the only evidence of attempted fraud, because no other fraud is proven, during the whole day of that election.

Now, the gentleman must not be offended if the vindication of the people, in this case, should expose the fact that leprosy and uncleanliness existed elsewhere. He must not be offended if the inquiry should arise whetner he belongs to that denomination of men, who, being without sin, are by special grace permitted to cast the first stone. [Laughter.]

But, sir, he comes here, they say, upon notice. Now, I am not going to argue about notice. I care nothing about notice. I wish to say here, as my people desire me to say, that we waive all legal and technical objections, for, notice or no notice, specification or no specification, law or no law, we desire to be judged by the facts of the case. Sir, were I capable of claiming a seat here to which I never had been elected, I should expect, as I would deserve, the derision and scorn of all honorable men.

Now, sir, I am charged with having received illegal votes. Does the gentleman produce a single witness who swears to having voted for me, who voted illegally? Not one. Does he produce a single witness who swears to his knowledge of a single illegal vote having been given by any person, and given for me? Not one. I defy him to show any such evidence. It is not on this record. It is all inference. It is hearsay. It is what Tom, Dick, and Harry have said about rag tag and *bob-tail*. It is not such evidence as can justly impeach the character of electors. Of what, then, does it consist? It consists of declarations of intention on the part of certain men, to become citizens since the election. Did they vote? What evidence is there of the fact, beyond the similarity of names upon the list of voters? There is none. Are any of them produced? Not one. There is the evidence of two other men, who swear to the fact of illegal voting, but did not know for whom they voted. But does the whole number thus claimed defeat my majority? Not at all. It still leaves me a majority of 16, and if you add the 13 illegal votes that this report admits the contestant to have received, it increases my majority to 29. There is no escaping this result.

Oh, but, says the gentleman, the witnesses would not attend; they would not obey the subpena which was issued by the United States commissioner. Ay! "thereby hangs a tale." Under the act of Congress any judge of a court of record is made, by the selection of the party, a United States commissioner. Does the gentleman select one in Montour county, where these irregularities are complained of, or fraud—if it pleases any gentleman to call it so, though no such thing is charged in the specification, and none actually occurred? Not at all. Does he take one from Columbia county? Not at all. Does he take one from Luzerne county, adjoining? Not at all. Does he take the first man even in Wyoming county—the most distant county? Not at all; but he takes the most remote man, and for what reason, we shall see hereafter. He goes to Danville with this judge. They stay at the same house, and, as is shown by this record, occupy the same bed chamber, sleeping, and eating inseparably together during the whole two weeks of this investigation. Yes, sir, during those two weeks they were together inseparably, and the judge was engaged a good portion of the time in taking the depositions or affidavits of witnesses, *ex parte*, before they were called upon the stand! That is proved, but I should not have alluded to it if the chairman of the committee had not spoken yesterday—not from what appears upon the record, but from representations that have been made to him—in regard to the character of this judge. I do not wish to expose them. I know that the office of the common hangman is the most odious and hateful in the world. I feel to-day as if I were a public executioner compelled by virtue of my office to nail upon the gibbet of public opinion, a convicted malefactor. If there be any resurrection from the foot of the gallows, which their own hands have reared, I commend them to your mercy.

Mr. ASHE. I merely wish to say that I particularly stated that I did not approve of the conduct of either of the commissioners. They both acted as if they had not a proper idea of what was the duty of a commissioner.

Mr. FULLER. I am very glad to hear the admission in regard to the contestant's commissioner, but Judge Cooper I am bound to defend, and there is no complaint that he did not discharge his duty. He is a capable, an honest, and a highly honorable man. I say this of the contestant's judge, that during that examination he rejected questions that were perfectly legal, and admitted questions that the committee themselves will decide were inadmissible. I say, further, that he permitted a drunken witness to swear, and then refused to take down his testimony as it was delivered. The honorable chairman of the committee endeavored to excuse him yesterday, upon the ground that judges of courts very often exclude the impertinent and irrelevant answers of witnesses. That is perfectly correct; but you must recollect that *you are the judges* in this case. A commissioner is not the judge—he has no judicial powers. How are you to understand the temper, appearance, and character of a witness, to know whether he be drunk or sober, a sensible man or a fool, unless you have his statement upon oath, as it is made before the commissioner? It is impossible. That is the only means you have of judging. The witnesses do not come before you, and you have no means of determining from their appearance as to their character and credibility. I think, therefore, upon reflection, the chairman of the committee will admit that he was wrong in that regard.

Well now, sir, I do not find fault with the contestant, because he slept with the judge. That, doubtless, is a matter of taste, in which you or I, Mr. Speaker, might respectfully differ from him. But I do insist that the judge should have "assumed a virtue if he had it not." I do say that there is no language of reproach sufficiently pungent to express your commentary upon the conduct of that judge. His behavior excited suspicion and public remark—in fact, became a matter of public comment in the papers. I read from the Berwick Telegraph, a Democratic paper published in the county of Columbia, within the district:

"THE CONTESTED-ELECTION CASE.—We publish this week the principal and most important part of the "testimony" taken at Danville on the part of the plaintiff in this case. A more ribald mass of unmeaning nonsense, dignified with the name of evidence, we have rarely seen strung together. A miserable object or two, suborned with rum and money—admitting, under oath, that they had been recently drinking in the room of the contestant, are brought forward and emptied of *hearsay* trash, that would not have been listened to as evidence for an instant by any body but the effigy of imbecility and ignorance, used as a tool, on the occasion, and called a 'commissioner.'"

There is such a thing as decorum, propriety, and decency, to be observed among judges, the absence of which cannot be too severely reproved. I make these remarks with much regret. The honorable contestant is alone responsible, for he has forced upon me the necessity thus to speak. Of Judge Jayne I desire to say that he is in good repute among his neighbors, and that I know nothing to his prejudice except his conduct in this case. It was discovered upon the first day of that examination that the subpena which had been issued by the gentleman, was irregular and illegal; that instead of issuing his process in the name of the United States of America, he had issued it in the name of the Commonwealth of Pennsylvania. Now, the Commonwealth of Pennsylvania has never passed a law authorizing *such* a subpena to be issued in her name; and no process can be issued in her name, except by the authority of her laws. But had the gentleman an opportunity to perfect it? Certainly he had. His examination lasted eight days. And a few days afterwards he gave me notice of his intention to hold a second examination, to examine the persons of whose non-attendance he had complained. Did he, then, perfect his process? Not at all. And, sir, it is believed that this subpena was issued in that form intentionally. I will not charge it, but I will state the reasons which have influenced others in coming to this opinion. The contestant stated before the committee, that he was a lawyer of twenty years' standing. Such is the fact, and I grant he has attained to some eminence in his profession. But having passed the *viginti annorum lucubrationes*, which, Blackstone says, are required to make a perfect lawyer, I submit that he was bound to know that his subpena was irregular and illegal. But if he did, as many believe, carry out this professional game of issuing an illegal subpena, in the first place, and then manage so to disgust people afterwards, as to prevent their attendance, I want to know if I am to be held accountable for the non-attendance of his witnesses? I want to know if this is to relieve him of the necessity of making out his case from evidence?

Now, I will show you in this connection what sort of evidence is regarded as proving an illegal voter. Here it is:

"Reuben Shock," a witness, to whom I will refer more at length hereafter, says:

"*Question.* Do you know L. Steinhammer, the Jewish rabbi?

"*Answer.* I do.

"*Q.* What do you know as to his voting at the election in October last, and who induced him to vote?

"*A.* I saw him about the court-house towards evening; I had some poplar scantling lying there which I went after, and saw several round him, and wanted him to vote—there were four, five, six, or eight standing there. I think Colonel Watson was one, and Dr. Strawbridge was another; they wanted him to vote, and he said he had no right to vote; they were coaxing him up to it, and gave him tickets. After that I saw him walking up to the box at the window, and saw his arm going up to the window; I thought his vote was pretty sure, that he had got it in, and I went away."

That is all the evidence we have about this man, except that his name appears upon the list of voters.

I will show you another:

"*Jacob Dietrick*, sworn.—*Question.* Was your brother David living in Danville borough at the time of the last October election?

"*Answer.* Yes.

"*Q.* How many years has he been in the United States?

"*A.* Next fall it was two years; it was one last October."

This is all the evidence we have about this man, except that a similar name appears upon the list of voters. He is not in any other way identified. Now, I want to know of the American Congress if evidence such as this is to disfranchise men? I want to know if men, freemen, American citizens, are to be disfranchised upon such stuff as that? Why, sir, in our courts of justice, in the most trivial matters between man and man, there is no security for truth without the sanctity of an oath; and will you in so important a matter as an election, involving the right of a freeman to the exercise of the highest and dearest right known under your Constitution—that of voting for his representative—will you undertake to disfranchise him upon such testimony as this? I submit it, sir;—I submit this question to the good sense and honest judgment of you all.

But there was another point which the gentleman raised before that committee, one which appeared most prominently in his specifications, which was this: He charges that the election officers had thrown out and suppressed votes, contrary to law. And how was this attempted to be shown? Why he produces a number of men to swear to the fact of having voted for him, whose votes, he says, were not counted in his favor, and almost the first person called was a Mr. George Smith. Well George swears positively and roundly that he voted for Mr. Wright, that he read his ticket, &c., &c. Upon his cross-examination we asked him if he could read—if he was sure he could read? Well, he said, he thought he could. We gave him a ticket with the word "Congress" upon it, and nothing else, and asked him to read it. After spelling for some five minutes (it was printed in large type) he said it read "Mr. Fuller" if it read anything. [Laughter.]

The next witness was a Mr. Daniel Whitmoyer—a very euphonious name. He swore that he voted for Mr. Wright; but upon being asked if he was sure he read his ticket, he replied that he could not read. [Renewed laughter.] Another witness was a Mr. Thomas Ray, who swore most positively and roundly that he voted for Mr. Wright. He said he voted a whole bunch for him, with a red string tied round it, [great laughter,] and that he had not voted for anybody else. And eighteen of the most respectable people of Danville swear that he has been a liar for the last twenty years, and that he is not to be believed under oath.

Again, a Mr. William Strow was called. He had been brought, as I understand, a distance of seventy-one miles by the contestant himself, for the purpose of testifying. The gentleman (Mr. Wright) is present, and can deny it if such was not the fact. He swears most roundly, too, that he voted for the contestant. We asked him who else he voted for? He stated he had voted for a man by the name of Thomas Yorks for constable. *There was no candidate for constable at that election.* We asked him, "Are you as certain that you voted for Mr. Wright for Congress, as you are that you voted for Mr. Yorks for constable?" "No, sir, I am not, because Mr. Yorks was the only man I cared a d——d about at the time of the election. [Great laughter.] All this you will find in this interesting volume of two hundred and ninety pages of evidence which you, Mr. Speaker, as a judge, and these judges, will of course read before they decide. Why, sir, at the request of the honorable chairman of this committee, this book was published; and for what purpose? The General Government has been at the expense of—I do not know how much, but certainly to a considerable amount—in its publication, and are you going to throw it under your table without reading it. [Laughter.] I undertake to say you will read every page from number one to two hundred and ninety. [Renewed laughter.] These are the intelligent "white freemen" whose votes the honorable contestant says were rejected. There is just one dozen of them, and if time would permit, I would introduce you to them all. You will find their names in the minority report. The committee were of opinion that where voting, as in Pennsylvania, is by secret ballot, this kind of testimony should be received with some caution—that to render it credible it should at least be intelligent, positive, and above suspicion. Judging the witnesses by this standard, they came to the conclusion that this part of the case was not sustained. I dismiss it, therefore, with the remark, that I wish to be distinctly understood as laying no claim to the suffrages of these *gentlemen*. I hope I have not any of that *kind of merit*—any of those *high qualities*, which could attract and attach to me men of this character. For these "most sweet voices" the honorable contestant and myself never will be rivals.

Now, sir, we come to the irregularity of the election, and this is the point to which I wish to direct the particular attention of the House, as it was the point to which the chairman of the committee (Mr. Ashe) especially addressed himself.

It is complained that Judge Kitchen, the judge of this election, stood at the window a good portion of the day, and received the ballots from the voters. This, says the chairman of the committee, was in violation of law, and designed to cloak a fraud; that his position, under the law, was that of umpire merely; that he was to sit in dignity, of course, from nine o'clock in the morning till seven o'clock in the evening, and could not interfere in any manner with the voters or the ballots unless the inspectors should disagree. Now, if the chairman had read a little further into the law, he would have discovered his error. I am happy to say, however, that the disposition he has manifested in this matter has been fair throughout, and I wish to say also that I do not complain of any of the committee. I have been treated fairly and with uniform courtesy by them all. I desire, above all, not to misrepresent him, and as he indulged me in interrupting him in his remarks yesterday, so he shall have the same privilege to-day, if you will only give me time enough to reply. [Laughter.] But I was proceeding to say, that if the chairman had read a little further he would have found that the form of oath for the judge of an election, prescribed by, and made part of the law, requires that he shall faithfully assist the inspectors in conducting the election. Assist in what? Why, certainly, assist in the discharge of any duty imposed upon the inspectors, in the reception, distribution, and counting the tickets, and in the general conduct and management of the election. This is the practice in Pennsylvania, and every member upon this floor from that State knows the fact. If they were to be tried upon the same ground, you could cut of all their heads to morrow. Not one would be entitled to a seat in this House if such an objection could be sustained. It is the uniform practice in Pennsylvania for the judges to assist in this manner. But in case there is a question about the reception of a vote, then he is charged with the higher and more extraordinary power of determining whether the voter be a qualified elector or not. Such is the law, and such is the practice in Pennsylvania.

But, sir, who was Judge Kitchen? For twenty years a resident of Danville. Twice elected sheriff of the county, an acting justice of the peace. In politics, a Democrat. In this case, however, he swears that he did not vote for either party. Judge Kitchen cloak a fraud! We could not have selected a more impartial, or a more unprejudiced man. Judge Kitchen cheat, and cheat for me! His whole life, his whole character, repels any such insinuation.

But who was Thomas Mettler? For he has been spoken of in this connection as a man who had some grains of honesty left? What does he say? Does he not swear that this election was conducted fairly and honestly? Does not he say that all was done in the presence of the whole board, and that it was fairly done? And is he not their witness? But, some months afterwards, Mr. Mettler, who is a fun-loving man, fond of cracking his "dry joke," declared to some men with whom he was indulging his natural humor, that he guessed "it was not all done exactly right. The fact was, they wanted Fuller elected so d—n badly that anybody could vote." [Laughter.] Now, we proved by several witnesses that this Mr. Mettler was in the habit of cracking this kind of jokes, yet this happening months after the election is brought in here to give an impression unfavorable to Mr. Mettler, and in prejudice of the election in this case. Yes, sir, as the gentleman at my right remarks, in violation of every principle of evidence. They cannot impeach their own witness; besides, fifteen of his neighbors were produced, who testified that he was a man of truth and integrity.

Another inspector in this election was Mr. McCallister, who has been for thirty-seven years a resident of Danville He swears the election was conducted fairly and honestly. In politics he is a Democrat, who voted for me.

I believe you will all pardon him for that; if you do not, he says he will do the same thing again. [Laughter.]

But, then, who is the clerk who is complained of in this case? Why Mr. E. W. Conklin. He is complained of because, during a portion of the time, he assisted the inspectors in the discharge of their duties. Why, nothing is more common than when the inspectors have to go out, as from necessity they sometimes must, during the nine hours of the election—they must eat and drink, and, being men, do such other things as nature requires. I say, when they go out nothing is more common than for the clerks to assist. Mr. Conklin did this in good faith, and he swears there was no fraud in the reception, in the distribution, or in the counting of the tickets. Who is Mr. Conklin? He is a Democrat. His only offence, too, is having voted for me; and I know you will pardon him for that. Now, sir, here a majority of the board were Democrats. The returning judges were Democrats, and they have returned me here, and I believe I hold this seat honestly. Where is the proof that I do not?

Now, sir, there was another point raised by the committee, which was this: They say there are eighty three names appearing upon the "list of voters," who do not appear upon the "list of taxables," and therefore they say, because the reason of their voting is not affixed to their names, they are to be regarded as illegal voters. Upon this point I most respectfully join issue, and I shall prove, I think, to the entire satisfaction of the committee, that they are entirely mistaken in this regard.

Now, sir, under the laws of Pennsylvania, as every Pennsylvanian here knows, there are two other classes of voters who may be qualified voters under the law, whose names do not appear upon the "taxable" or "register's" list. Those are voters between the ages of twenty one and twenty-two years; and those who have paid a tax within the State of Pennsylvania within the period of two years, and have resided for the period of ten days in the election district where they offer to vote. Now, sir, this very point is ruled expressly in the case of *Littell vs. Robbins*—a case upon which I think the chairman of the Committee on Elections [Mr. Ashe] served as a member—and I find, in the report of that case, this language:

"Under the laws of Pennsylvania persons are entitled to vote whose names are not on that list, (the list of taxables,) if they have been residents of the State one year, and ten days immediately preceeding the election in the district, and have paid within two years a State or county tax, assessed at least ten days before the election.' Citizens of the United States, also, who are between the age of twenty-one and twenty-two, who have resided within the State one year, and within the district ten days, are entitled to vote, although they have not been assessed, or paid taxes, and their names are not on the list. *Under these provisions of the law, many persons vote at every election whose names do not appear on the registered lists.*"

"Under these provisions of law," said Mr. Ashe, the chairman of this committee—"Under these provisions of the law many persons vote at every election, whose names do not appear upon the "register list.'"

Now, sir, I submit, if in the case of Littell *vs.* Robbins, a Pennsylvania case, it was expressly ruled by the committee, "that under these provisions of the law many persons vote at every election, whose names do not appear upon the register's list," whether they can be correct now, when they say that these eighty three names must be regarded as illegal voters? Clearly, most clearly they are mistaken.

Is it too much to suppose, that under these provisions of the law of Pennsylvania, citizens, qualified voters, should have voted in the borough of Danville, who were not upon the list of taxables, and still be legal voters? And are not you, the judges, bound to regard them as legal voters until they are proved to be otherwise? Where is the proof? I challenge its production.

Again, the committee in the case of Littell *vs.* Robbins say that the "register list," which the law of Pennslvania requires the assessor to take every year, is the best evidence of the number of electors in the district, though incomplete, for the reasons above stated. Now, in the borough of Danville there are returned the names of 731 voters only, while the list of "taxables" embraces the names of 1,231. Here, in the borough of Danville, against which complaint is made that this was an extraordinary vote, we see that there were 500 more persons "*prima facie*" entitled to vote; while in the case of Littell *vs.* Robbins, where there was a much larger poll, the excess was only 295, so that this comparison is very greatly in our favor.

Ah, but, said the gentleman (Mr. Ashe) yesterday, this poll had been divided into two districts, and there was a greater number of votes in 1850 than in 1849-'51. But what does that prove, sir? Does that prove fraud? I venture to assert that this year there will be 300,000 more votes polled in this country than there was last year, and 300,000 more this year than there will be next year. And will you disfranchise the 300,000 voters for the reason stated by the chairman of the committee? You cannot do that, sir. Such a conclusion cannot be justified. His error is too glaring for argument.

Now there is another thing about these 83 names. None of these men were produced. Not one of them. All the evidence you have of them, is from this comparison of the lists of taxables and voters. Now, I want to know if the orthography of clerks is to be regarded as conclusive in this matter; that is the only evidence produced? Here we show you 26 names—*George Kinn* on the list of voters, and *George King* on the list of taxables. We show you the name of *John D. Long* upon one list, with a capital D in the middle of his name, and *John Delong* upon the other list Also, the names of 26 others, bearing a like resemblance. And yet, without identifying one of the 83 complained of, they are to be regarded as illegal voters.

Are these men to be disfranchised upon such evidence as this? Why, sir, you might as well deny your own identity, if you should chance to see your own name, Mr. Speaker, spelled *Bogg* on the register of one of the hotels instead of Boyd. These things, similar mistakes, happen every day, as you and all of us know; and may not the clerks have erred in writing down the names of the voters?

[Here the hammer fell.]

Mr. DUNCAN. It is, I believe, the unanimous wish of this House to allow the gentleman (Mr. Fuller) to proceed in his argument in this case.

Mr. LETCHER. I objected yesterday to the chairman of the committee going on beyond his hour, and I gave notice that I should object to a departure from the rules of the House. I therefore feel bound to object to the gentleman's proceeding.

JUNE 26, 1852.

Mr. DAVIS, of Massachusetts, having the floor, inquired of the sitting member whether the 11th Congressional district of Pennsylvania was a Whig or a Democratic district; also in regard to the decisions of the courts of Pennsylvania relating to the duties of inspectors, &c.

Mr. FULLER. In reply to the interrogatory of the gentleman from Massachusetts, I will state, that on yesterday the honorable contestant alleged that during the last ten years this, the eleventh Congressional district of Pennsylvania had, in consequence of the course pursued by the Democratic paper, (the Wilkesbarre Farmer,) and the disorganizing band which I had about me, been Whig in its politics. All that he says I know. I differ from the honorable gentleman entirely.

He says again, "that it is not a Democratic district, and cannot be a Democratic district, so long as these wholesale frauds are permitted to exist that have existed for the last ten years." Let us see if this be so. My recollection of the history and political character of the district and its representatives is this: From 1840 to 1844, the eleventh district was represented by the Hon. Benjamin A, Bidlack. I wish to know from my colleague (Mr. Ross) if he was a Democrat.

Mr. ROSS. He was, sir.

Mr. FULLER. However the contestant may have regarded him, it is certain that Mr. Polk, upon his elevation to the Presidency, expressed his high confidence by sending him abroad as Chargé to New Grenada. He had been elected to Congress from this district at two successive elections, by majorities varying from 2,000 to 3,000, and was the regular Democratic nominee. From 1844 to 1846, that district was represented by Hon. Owen D. Leib. I wish to know from the same gentleman if he was a Democrat?

Mr. ROSS. I cannot answer the gentleman's question. I have no personal knowledge of Mr. Leib or his politics.

Mr. FULLER. There are other gentlemen here who know the fact. He was elected over Mr. Butler, Whig, and over another Democratic competitor, by a handsome majority. He was the regular Democratic nominee. Was the gentleman from Tennessee (Mr. JONES) acquainted with Mr. Leib?

Mr. JONES. Yes, sir, I was.

Mr. FULLER. Was he a Democrat?

Mr. JONES. He was so received here, I believe.

Mr. FULLER. I suppose that is not a matter of doubt at all. He was a very worthy, honest, honorable man, and a good Democrat. That brings us up to 1846. In 1846, sir, Mr. Butler, owing to his great personal popularity, and owing to that great storm, both of politics and the physical elements, which swept over Pennsylvania, was elected over Mr. Leib; and he owed his election, in some degree, as I have understood, to the very earnest and highly-commendable efforts of, as it was claimed, the gentleman contestant and his friends. It was affirmed at the next election in 1848 that Mr. Butler had acted in bad faith, because he ran against the honorable contestant, (*then, as now, a consistent national Democrat*) because the honorable contestant and his friends had secured the election of Mr. Butler over Mr. Leib in 1846. As it is notorious throughout the District that Mr. Butler was never *forgiven* by the honorable contestant for this offence, he may desire to explain why. It gives me pleasure to afford him the opportunity now.

But he charged yesterday that the district had been misrepresented for ten years through fraud and the disorganizers. Who committed the fraud? Who were the disorganizers then? Yet he charges the tried and true Democracy there with being disorganized, when Mr. Butler was elected, as I am informed he has ever claimed, through his instrumentality and that of his friends. I wish to know, and he can answer, if publicly, at Sunbury, in the presence of the supreme judges there, and at other places, he has not made this public declaration, or if his friends have not made it for him? I am thus particular in referring to the matter in order to refresh his memory in this regard, and that I may not misrepresent him, for my only object is to vindicate the truth of history. Why, sir, he said on yesterday, as I understood him—such at least seemed to be his implication—that Hon. Andrew Beaumont had been elected during the ten years named, and that he was not a Democrat. I ask Mr. Ross if he was and is not a Democrat?

Mr. ROSS. Yes, sir, he was and is a Democrat—sound and radical.

Mr. FULLER. But he was very much mistaken in the time of his service. Mr. Beaumont was elected in 1832, and remained until 1836. At his first election he was elected over two competitors—Dr. Thomas W. Minor, a Federalist, and James McClintock, a highly-estimable Democrat.

In 1848, the contestant ran against Mr. Butler and Mr. Samuel P. Collings. Mr. Butler was elected. Mr. Collings had received the regular nomination from the Democracy of Luzerne, the county in which all the candidates resided, and one exceedingly prolific in that material.

As Mr. Collings was charged with being a spurious candidate at that election, I submit the following manifesto, published at the time in the Carbondale Democrat, which fully vindicates his political reputation:

"THE CONGRESSIONAL CONFERENCE.—The conferees selected by the Democratic Convention of the three counties composing our (eleventh) Congressional district, met at Wilkesbarre, on Saturday last The three conferees of Luzerne were instructed for Mr Collings; two from Columbia for Colonel Wright; and Wyoming, though according to the equitable ratio established by the last conference only entitled to one, persisted in having two, who were also instructed for Colonel Wright. The question turning on the admission of the second delegate from Wyoming, and adhering to the ratio adopted at the last conference, the conference split, the three Luzerne conferees *unanimously* nominated Mr. Collings, and the conferees from the other two counties unanimously nominated Colonel Wright. Thus matters stand, and we much regret that they are in such a shape. A difficult and unpleasant question presents itself to us and the Democracy of Luzerne. Which of the candidates shall receive our suffrages and support? In this county, where both are known, the ability and competency of both candidates are universally admitted. In this respect, to neither of these or the Whig candidate can any exceptions be taken. Upon other considerations the question must be decided. Now we believe that in this matter, *the Democracy of Luzerne have a duty to perform toward themselves.* If our sister counties persist in claiming the right to select the candidate when it belongs to *them*, and also when it belongs to *us*, we should like to know before we go any further, upon what prerogative it is based? This is not the first time the Democracy of Luzerne have been *overruled* in the same manner by the *dictation* of Columbia. If the decisions of our conventions, the selections made by them when they have an *undoubted right to select*, and when the candidates presented are of *undoubted* Democracy, *integrity*, and ability, are to be utterly and causelessly repudiated, and everything reversed by the beck of *self constituted dictators*, 'we will either submit to it or else we wont.' If we submit to it we will let others do our whole business for us, without going through with useless formalities on our part; if not, we will endeavor, so far as in us lies, *to carry out the decision of our own conventions* when it is proper that they should be respected, and by every principle of comity and reciprocity control the Congressional conference. In this manner did the decision and nomination of the Columbia convention rightfully and with our full acquiescence control the Congressional question in '46. The candidate was not our choice; but it was our choice that Columbia should make *her own selection*, and hence our concurrence.

"It was now *our right* to make our *selection*; we have done so, and Columbia and Wyoming should have ratified that selection. Every principle of reciprocity required it; our undeviating adherence to their rights and privileges in like cases required it. So palpable a *disregard* of the *expressed wishes* of our Democracy, and so wanton an attempt to victimize one every way worthy of that partiality, which the delegates assembled in our convention expressed, is without an excuse. This attempt at dictation comes with a bad grace, in a bad time, and may defeat the candidate that should have received the unanimous support of the Democracy of this district this fall; but it may result in ultimate good. Our convention has made their choice, the Congressional conference should have ratified it unanimously. We are prepared to do our duty, as we conceive it, toward the Democracy of Luzerne, in supporting heartily the nomination of our convention and the rights of our county."

Now, yesterday he charged Colonel Best, a Democrat, with a highly heinous offence, because, when a member of the State Senate, he voted for himself. Let us understand the facts. In 1847 he was elected to the State Senate. At the opening of the session of 1849 there happened to be sixteen whigs and seventeen democrats. It was impossible that any election could be secured or that body organized, unless some Democrat voted for himself, and Mr. Best, by the instructions of many of his constituents, voted for himself; but in doing so he did no more than the present worthy Democratic Governor of Pennsylvania did for himself in our State Senate on a previous occasion. I ask Mr. Ross if that is not the case.

Mr. ROSS. I am not able to answer the question, for I have no knowledge of it.

Mr. FULLER. Other gentlemen know the fact. I know it. I do not wish to be understood as complaining of him; he doubtless did right. Although not elected Speaker, he has since been elected Governor, and received last year in this contested district three thousand one hundred and ninety six majority. He is an accomplished gentleman, and possesses in a high degree the confidence of his party. Where were the disorganizers then? Why, sir, at this very contested election of which the contestant so bitterly complains of disorganizers and of fraud, a Democratic Canal Commissioner, a Democratic Auditor General, and a Democratic Surveyor General received majorities varying from two thousand to three thousand in this district. None of THEM were cheated. Why, at this very election district, at this very Danville poll of which he complains, Charles R. Buckalew, an able and distinguished Democrat, ran for the State Senate; and while he received but two votes, Mr. Wright received thirty-two at this poll; yet Mr. Buckalew was elected by over fifteen hundred majority. Was he cheated? No other man seems to have been cheated but the honorable contestant—certainly no other candidate has ever complained. At this election Col. Best received over thirteen hundred majority in his own county, a highly gratifying evidence of the confidence of his neighbors.

Sir, the honorable gentleman yesterday declined to respond to what he was pleased to denominate my personal charges. He expressed a regret, which he felt "deeply, keenly, and sensibly," that I had turned this into a personal controversy. He declined, however, for a special reason. He would not recriminate "out of regard for the sitting member's father." I am happy to learn that one of my family has enjoyed his distinguished consideration, and he will permit me to express the hope, that if he was withheld yesterday by the love he bore my father, that the same restraining influence will hereafter control his pen and his private conversation.

Not to be outdone in courtesy on this occasion, I desire, in all sincerity, to express the high regard I entertain for his father. He, too, is a "worthy, amiable, and upright man."

Neither of them were public men. They always preferred that "post of honor, the private station;" their children have sadly degenerated. While I do not recognize the propriety of introducing our ancestors to the distinguished attention of the

"American Congress," still, as the honorable gentleman has done me the courtesy in the one case, I could do no less than return the compliment in the other. My regret is that the son should, in this instance, have so widely departed from what I believe would have been the advice and example of his worthy sire.

But, sir, I have no desire to make this matter personal; none whatever. I alluded to the fact and to the circumstances of his defeat in 1848, because he had spoken of it himself to the committee; and to do him full justice, I quoted what I supposed to be his own version of the facts. I spoke of his behavior before the return judges, because that exhibition was part of the history of the case. Let it all pass. I will be more amiable in future. There is another matter in regard to which I must *correct* the gentleman. He stated that the journal from which I read yesterday, was not the leading Democratic paper in the county of Luzerne. Now, I affirm that it is, and am prepared to show that, for twenty-odd years, before even his earliest dream of Democracy, it was, and ever since has been, the leading Democratic paper of the county. I have the papers here showing that it has always uniformly supported the regular nominee of the Democratic party, and that, too, at times, if I mistake not, when he has been engaged in their butchery. I dislike to revive too many unpleasant recollections. I will simply remind him of 1839, 1844, and 1846; and yet these men—its editors—are charged with being disorganizers, because they are personal friends of mine, and for no other reason in the world, that I can understand.

The honorable contestant dedicated a good portion of his speech to Messrs. Hancock and Foley, whom he classically denominated "*the nabobs of a pig iron mill.*" He informed us they had failed, and *the smoke of their furnaces was just disappearing*. I marked with regret his look and voice of exultation. If they have been unsuccessful it is a public misfortune, for many an honest hard-working man must be turned away whom their energies and enterprize have furnished with profitable employment. Let me commend to the *earnest* consideration of the honorable genman that divine precept, "forgive your enemies." Its practice will make him more comfortable here, and I hope happier hereafter.

I wish to refer, very briefly, to a point in the argument of the gentleman. He endeavored to convey the impression that Judge Kitchen was a dishonest man, an unfair judge, by reading just one question and one answer, and no more, from his printed testimony. It was this:

"*Question.* Was or was not the election fairly and honestly conducted?

"*Answer.* After the tickets came in, it was all fairly and honestly conducted, as far as I know."

To that extent he read—no further, as you and all here will remember. Just listen, if you please, to the questions and answers which follow immediately thereafter:

"*Question.* Did you receive a ticket from any person that you knew was not a legal voter?

"*Answer.* We did not.

"*Q.* Have you any knowledge of any fraud committed by any of the officers in the reception, distribution, or counting of the tickets?

"*A.* I have not. I did not see anything like it."

And yet the gentleman with the book in his hand read but the one question, and then proceeded to comment in such language as would make this House infer that Judge Kitchen did not manfully, and openly, and decidedly declare that there was no fraud committed. I ask if that be fair—if that be candid?

Another thing; in order to impress this House unfavorably with regard to Judge Kitchen, he stated a conversation that had occurred between Judge Kitchen and Mr. Smith B. Thompson, to this effect, that when the local question was affected, they let almost anybody vote if he was only large enough; and the impression, if not intended, was conveyed, that this conversation took place with reference to this very election. Was not that your impression, Mr. Speaker? I ask gentlemen of this House if that was not their impression? And yet if you look to the testimony of Smith B Thompson, you will see that that conversation occurred in 1848—two years before this election. Thus are conversations long prior to this election *lugged* in at this length of time, unfavorably to impress this House with regard to the conduct and character of this man, and the conduct and character of this election.

And now, sir, with reference to these eighty-three voters of which complaint is made, I propose fully to satisfy this House—as I think I can do—that they were fair and honest electors, and that not one of them has been impeached. Why, you find upon examination that the number is reduced by the comparison of names to fifty-seven, and the only complaint which remains against those men—because none of them are produced—is, that the word "tax" does not appear after their names on the list of voters. That is the only complaint against them, and for that reason, says the gentleman, they are to be regarded as illegal voters. I have shown that under the law of Pennsylvania persons resident within the State one year, who have paid State or county taxes, whether in or out of the district, and who are not on the register's list, are nevertheless qualified voters, if they were residents of the district ten days before the election. It is in evidence that in the borough of Wilkesbarre, with a poll of four hundred and fourteen votes, there were thirty-one taxed voters. The borough of Danville polled seven hundred and thirty-one votes, and the same proportion would give them fifty-seven, which is the precise number to which we reduced these names by a comparison of lists. And yet it is urged that because the word "tax" does not appear, they are, therefore, to be regarded as illegal voters.

Just listen one moment, if you please, to what the courts of Pennsylvania have said on this very question. In the case of Skerrett, irregularities of this character were complained of, and decided by the courts. I believe the chairman of the committee thought the case was not exactly in point. But I will satisfy him that it is. In that case it was complained that all the directory provisions of the seventy-third section of the law of Pennsylvania, relating to elections, had been disregarded. The courts decided that they were simply directory to the officers of the election, and that a failure to observe them could not vitiate or set aside the election.

If the courts of Pennsylvania, considering the very irregularity of which complaint is made here, have thus regarded them, will you not, in a Pennsylvania case, depending upon the construction of her laws, pay some respect to the decisions of her courts?

Now, I undertake to say, that not in one township out of twenty in that district does the word "tax" appear after the names of voters. I hold in my hand a certificate of five election districts, giving the contestant three hundred majority, in which the clerk of the court certifies that he has carefully examined these lists, and the word "tax" does not appear against a single name. There are four districts, mentioned in the evidence itself, in which the same omission appears. It is a common, an almost universal omission in Pennsylvania, and I appeal to every gentleman from Pennsylvania on this floor to say if such is not the fact.

Mr. McNAIR. I can say that I think it is not the case in my district.

Mr. FULLER. Then, you are an exception, and I am very happy to learn that there is one gentleman from Pennsylvania who is entitled to his seat. I do not think there is any other gentleman here who will say the same thing; if there be let him speak—we will make some inquiry after our colleagues' credentials hereafter.

Now, I do not contend, nor can any Pennsylvanian here contend, that the elections in that State are held in strict and literal compliance with the law. Why, the object of the directory provisions of every election law is to secure a fair expression of the legal vote, a fair expression of the popular will; and whatever tends to narrow, contract, or in any way to abridge the rights of the voters must be avoided. It would be highly desirable that our elections should be held and conducted by our most intelligent men—by men most familiar with the laws; but this is impossible. We must, from the necessity of things, depend upon the common intelligence, and the common integrity of men; and all that we can expect or require is a substantial compliance with the law. That there was a substantial compliance in this case—that no fraud was committed at this election, I do positively aver, and that upon the most positive testimony. That some illegal votes were given, is possibly true; but that the result was not changed or affected thereby, is conclusively shown.

Mr. Speaker, I hold in my hand the certificate of my election, signed by all the return judges of the 11th Congressional District. I hold also the proclamation of the Governor of Pennsylvania, under the broad seal of the Commonwealth. I stand here a *free*, untrammelled, *elected* representative of the *people*. I ask no favor. I "shall not crook the pregnant hinges of the knee that thrift may follow fawning." I make no political appeals; but in my place this day I claim for my people the constitutional right of choosing for themselves, and I demand your affirmation of their election.

Here the hammer fell, the hour having expired.

www.ingramcontent.com/pod-product-compliance
Lightning Source LLC
LaVergne TN
LVHW020643110826
845149LV00004B/1338

* 9 7 8 1 4 1 8 1 9 0 4 4 6 *